Fat Daisy

Inner Beauty Secrets from a Real Dog

Beverly West and Jason Bergund

Photographs by Jessica Alonso

Andrews McMeel Publishing, LLC

Kansas City

Acknowledgments

We would like to thank our brilliant editor, Patty Rice, for taking such good care of Fat Daisy, and helping her shine from the inside out. Thanks also to Katie Anderson, Julie Barnes, Diane Marsh, and our incomparable agent, Jenny Bent. We would also like to thank Rosanna Inc. (www.rosannainc.com) for their charming tableware, and Connie Alonso and her People's Choice Thrift Store (770-537-0009) for her imaginative props and retro-doggie wear, not to mention the s'mores. Thanks, Mom! Finally, a very special thanks to our very own Fat Daisy, the smartest, cutest, and roundest Chihuahua in New York City, who has taught us so many important lessons about life and love and the joys of empty calories.

06 07 08 09 10 WKT 10 9 8 7 6 5 4 3 2 1

ISBN-13: 978-0-7407-6154-6
ISBN-10: 0-7407-6154-4

Library of Congress Control Number: 2006923215

www.andrewsmcmeel.com

Book design by Diane Marsh

Meet Fat Daisy

Fat Daisy is a toy Chihuahua who outgrew her teacup after the birth of her four puppies. Daisy never did quite drop the baby weight and regain her girlish figure. In fact, it's probably safe to say that there has never been a Chihuahua quite as fat as Fat Daisy.

Fat Daisy has experienced the heartache of upper thigh spread, of pinching way more than an inch around the middle, and outgrowing even her fat jeans. And like so many of us, despite bravely enduring the barren and treatless world of crash diets, the rigors of radical fitness regimens, and the disillusionment of failed fad supplements, Fat Daisy was still fat.

But then one day while counting calories on her favorite pillow, Fat Daisy saw the light, and the secrets that she discovered are helping her win her battle of the bulge and look and feel her best by living each day to the fullest.

Now, in her up-close and personal weight loss journal of words and pictures from a real dog who's been there and done that, Fat Daisy shares her inner beauty secrets with all of us who struggle with our own inner Fat Daisies. She spreads the good word about her fitness regimen of confidence, enthusiasm, a positive self-image, a good sense of humor, a zest for living, and lots and lots of unconditional love.

Fat Daisy comforts us all that we are only as beautiful as we think we are. She reminds Fat Daisies everywhere that the best cure for the bad-body-image blues is to laugh at our fears, live without limits, and count our blessings instead of our calories, one Fat Daisy at a time.

Everybody has those days
when they feel like Fat Daisy.

Like when your tiara slips

or your bubble bursts

or your Daisy Dukes shrink in the wash

or you're just feeling too huge to hula.

We all go through periods when we
feel a little bloated and blue.

And we all know it's hard to get back in the race when you feel like a pumpkin with legs,

and you can't keep up in the fast lane when you feel like a sidecar on the Vespa of life.

At first, Daisy was in denial and tried to compensate with oversized frocks, flamboyant hats, and creative draping.

But, finally, Daisy took a long look at herself
and realized that unless she stood on her tiptoes,
her belly was definitely brushing the ground.
And then, like many of us, Daisy panicked and
went looking for a quick fix.

Fat Daisy tried the Grapefruit Diet

and then the Cabbage Soup Diet

and the Olive Oil Diet

and one diet where she ate
nothing but Swedish Fish.

Fat Daisy did eight minutes in the morning

and tried to resist the temptation
to snack late at night.

She battled the urge to splurge
around the holidays.

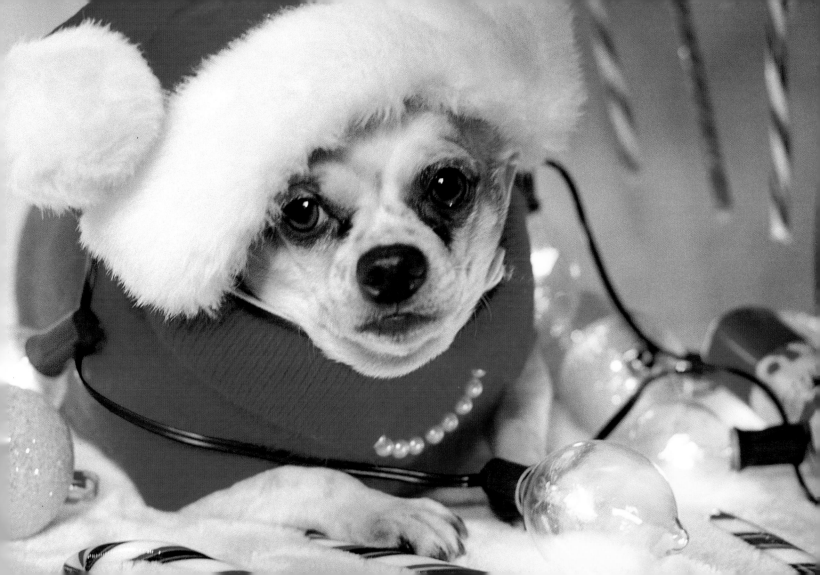

Fat Daisy even spent a
few weeks in South Beach.

She visited the Eiffel Tower of Treats
to see why French dogs don't get fat.

Next, Daisy headed west to Sonoma

and dieted with the stars in Hollywood.

Fat Daisy even enlisted in Oprah's Boot Camp

and then, when all else failed, TrimSpa Daisy!

But although Daisy had a shake for breakfast and a shake for lunch

and drank lots of green tea

and put Jenny on speed-dial

and did her best to always eat all her greens,

(though they were usually on top of
a cheeseburger and next to a side of fries),
Fat Daisy was still fat.

And somehow, no matter how many carbs Daisy cut, she always seemed to wind up at the bottom of a big bowl of pasta.

And then one day, quite unexpectedly,
while counting calories on her favorite pillow,
Fat Daisy saw the light.

She realized that maybe feeling beautiful
could be about as easy as following your nose as
long as you remembered a few simple rules:

Find the courage to leave your comfort zone and think outside your box.

Look in the mirror and make friends with who you are, rather than seeing only who you are not.

Cultivate a circle of support.

Stop playing yo-yo with your metabolism.

And try not to eat anything that
is bigger than your head.

Take a little time each day
to dream in the sunshine

and a little more time to
trot through a field of clover.

And, most important, remember that no matter what the scale says, with the magic wand of love, enthusiasm, humor, and self-confidence, even a Fat Daisy can sprout wings and fly.